Loved

And Fully Surrendered

Copyright ©2025 Barbara De Simon

Published in Windsor, Ontario, Canada by Barbara De Simon and makeyourselfready.com–a Kingdom ministry equipping women to fulfill their call to advance the Kingdom in their sphere of influence.

All rights reserved. This book is protected by the copyright laws of Canada. No part of this publication may be reproduced, stored in a retrieval system, or transmitted in any form or by any means–electronic, mechanical, photocopy, recording or any other–except for brief quotations, without prior permission of the author/publisher.

Unless otherwise noted, scripture quotations are from the New King James Version®. Copyright © 1982 by Thomas Nelson, Inc. Used by permission. All rights reserved.

Scripture quotations marked TPT are from The Passion Translation®. Copyright © 2017, 2018, 2020 by Passion & Fire Ministries, Inc. Used by permission. All rights reserved. ThePassionTranslation.com.

Scripture quotations marked NLT are taken from the Holy Bible, New Living Translation, copyright 1996, 2004.

Scripture quotations identified as NIV® are from the New International Version®. Copyright © 1973, 1978, 1984, 2011 by Biblica, Inc.™ Used by permission. All rights reserved worldwide.

Cover and interior design by Barbara De Simon
Cover image from iStock.com

ISBN: 978-1-7383840-3-7

"Comfort, yes, comfort My people!"
Says your God.
"Speak comfort to Jerusalem, and cry out to her,
That her warfare is ended,
That her iniquity is pardoned;
For she has received from the LORD's hand
Double for all her sins."
The voice of one crying in the wilderness:
"Prepare the way of the LORD;
Make straight in the desert
A highway for our God.
Every valley shall be exalted
And every mountain and hill brought low;
The crooked places shall be made straight
And the rough places smooth;
The glory of the LORD shall be revealed,
And all flesh shall see it together;
For the mouth of the LORD has spoken."
Isaiah 40:1-5

Dedicated

To my good friend
Rosie Wagner
and all our good friends at
Abba's Girls–A Planting of the Lord.
I cou dn't do it without you.
I love you all.

Table of Contents

1 ~ Where it all Began ~ 1

2 ~ All of Nothing ~ 5

3 ~ Saved and Empowered ~ 15

4 ~ Holy Spirit ~ 24

5 ~ Journey to Wholeness ~ 33

6 ~ Stumbling Blocks Removed ~ 39

7 ~ Freedom in Christ ~ 49

Conclusion ~ 59

About the Author ~ 60

References ~ 62

1

Where it all Began

I was roughly fifteen years old when my high school held a concert with a Foreigner tribute band and they played my most favorite Foreigner song called, *I Wanna Know What Love Is*. I loved that song.

At fifteen years of age, this was the cry of my heart. Not only did the band do a great job, but the lead singer also wasn't bad looking. In fact, he was quite cute, and my fifteen-year-old heart was smitten. It felt a little like love, or so I thought, so I sat in that feeling for several days. At home I played my "45" vinyl record[1] of that song repeatedly–over and over, swaying to the music, imagining an epic slow dance with my latest crush.

Why did I not know what love was? Well, that was a very good question. After all, I had a fairly stable home life. Mom and dad stayed together though there *was* a threat of

---

[1] For you younger folk, a "45" vinyl record was a small record containing just one hit song in comparison to a full album containing many songs.

divorce spoken once or twice. I had siblings and a few close friends. We went to church. So, what was missing? Unfortunately, there was a lot missing including emotional health and support, but two other major things stand out that I will expand on. First, there was a big disconnect between what my parents said and what they did; my parents told me they loved me, but their actions at times did not support their words. This left me confused about what love was and what it should look like. Secondly, we *did* go to church, but it wasn't a Christian church that understood the greatest act of love ever known to mankind: the willing laying down of one's life for another. This of course was demonstrated by Jesus when He was brutally beaten almost to death and crucified on a cross to pay the penalty of our sin–to set us free from every work of darkness.

Our family went to a Christian Science church which does not recognize the sinful nature of man, nor does it recognize Jesus as divine. We knew God the Father existed and was very real and active in the lives of people, but we attempted to know God without first knowing and worshipping Jesus. I know now that our attempt was mostly unfruitful but at the time, I knew nothing of why Jesus was crucified; that piece of the whole puzzle of faith and life and God was missing. In fact, I knew that the puzzle just was not working. The pieces were not fitting together.

One day as the music of Foreigner rang out from my bedroom, my father desperately burst through my door saying, "Don't you know that God loves you?!" And I was just as confused! Because yes, I had been told a million times in Sunday School and at home. I knew it in my head, BUT I had never felt it in my heart, personally. I had never felt God's love in my heart for ME. The words "I love you" or "God loves you" had no power. They did not prove themselves to be true because there was no *evidence* of it. At some point, I *needed* my mental knowledge to become *experiential* knowledge in order to truly believe it and know it in my heart.

Gary Chapman talks about love languages—behaviors that communicate love in action, like words of affirmation, acts of service, physical touch, quality time, and gift giving. Those are great but there's one thing I think communicates love even more effectively and that is sacrifice. When someone is willing to sacrifice something for you or to give something up: *this* is when you know they truly prefer you over themselves. And this we know is the ultimate way Jesus and God the Father demonstrated His love for us; He willingly gave up His very life for us so we could be with Him forever.

When I was young, I didn't sense the love of God for me because first, I didn't know I needed forgiveness and second, I didn't know Jesus's sacrifice for me. Jesus is the door. Jesus is the gate for the sheep (John 10:9), His people. Jesus said in John 14:6, "I am the way, the truth, and the life. No one comes to the Father except through Me." So even though we believed in God, we did not truly know God because we had not come to Him through the ONLY legitimate way—through Jesus. It wasn't until I surrendered to the truth of Who Jesus really is and accepted Him as my Lord and Savior that I truly felt the deep love of God expressed for me in my heart. I finally knew that I knew, experientially, that He loved me.

    I sat on the bed with my sister praying a prayer of surrender and in the Spirit, as I confessed my need for forgiveness in repentance, a warm sensation like liquid love poured out over my head and the weight of my guilt lifted off my heart. And I thought, *THIS is what love is! This is what it's supposed to feel like. God REALLY does love me.*

2

All or Nothing

In Galatians 5:1 Paul says, "It is for freedom that Christ has set us free." Praise the Lord. However, this freedom and salvation do not become our reality until we surrender <u>everything</u> to the Lordship of Christ. Stating to one of the teachers of the law as being the most important commandment, Jesus said in Mark 12:30, "Love the Lord your God with all your heart and with all your soul and with all your mind and with all your strength.'" In other words, with your whole self—with every piece—every aspect of who you are needs to be submitted to God.

    Mental ascent of or intellectual agreement to the gospel is not enough for us to be saved or to make us Christians. Some of us began to go to church because someone won us over in an intellectual argument or convinced us that it was the "right" thing to do, but we may not have experienced the presence nor power of God in our lives. If this is true, it's possible (now don't shoot the messenger) that we don't even know God! Sorry, but attending church does not make us a Christ follower which is what the word "Christian" really means.

Do you remember the parable of the ten virgins in Matthew 25? Let's go there for a moment. The parable of the ten virgins is a story Jesus told about five wise virgins and five foolish virgins to teach us about the Kingdom of God and how things will go down at His second coming. The ten virgins all went out to meet the bridegroom as He was said to be arriving shortly. The bridegroom is a representation of Jesus. The ten virgins are representative of *believers* in the Kingdom of God. The lamp represents the heart. Matthew 25:1-2 says, "Then the kingdom of heaven shall be likened to ten virgins who took their lamps and went out to meet the bridegroom. Now five of them were wise, and five were foolish."

The difference between the wise and the foolish virgins was that the foolish did not take *extra* oil with them just in case the bridegroom took longer to arrive than expected or wanted. They assumed the bridegroom was coming *soon* (according to their definition). They failed to discern the times and prepare for delay. They were presumptuous and they did not discern the direction of the Lord to bring extra oil. Verse twelve tells us why. Jesus said to them, "Assuredly, I say to you, I do not know you" (Matt. 25:12b).

Here we have a story of ten virgins–five who were *disciples* of Jesus and in *relationship* with Him hearing His voice and five who only thought they belonged to Him but tragically did not. The truth was–they had no intimacy with the Lord–no desire in their heart for Him. No oil in their lamp meant no flame and no fire. Their passion had gone out. It's possible these five represent those in the church who are just waiting for the rapture so they can get out of here and they're weary from waiting. It's also possible that they represent those who have only accepted the gospel mentally without surrendering their ALL to Him and therefore have no fire on the altar of their heart.

Truthfully, we do not come into relationship with Christ until we repent and our agreement to the gospel includes the complete surrender of our heart., mind, will, emotions, thoughts and behaviours. We cannot hold anything back. Jesus gave His ALL for us and so we must reciprocate in kind to Him. He purchased all of who we are, in fullness, including our attitudes, opinions, perspectives, problems, habits, hangups, strengths and weaknesses–our love lives, our parenting lives, work lives, and leisure lives. Everything.

How do we come to a place of surrender to the Lord and what does repentance really mean? Well, let's consider surrender first.

Surrender

What is surrender? I asked Google and here is what I got from AI as an answer to the question, "What is the spiritual meaning of surrender?"

> "In a spiritual context, surrender means to release the struggle for control, trusting in a higher power ... to guide events and your own

actions. It involves a conscious choice to yield your personal will, not as a passive act of giving up, but as a powerful affirmation of faith in a larger plan. This practice fosters inner freedom, facilitates personal growth, and can lead to states of peace and resilience by reducing resistance to challenges and allowing for deeper acceptance of what is present."

From this quote I think the concept of "releasing the struggle for control," and "yielding your personal will" are two very key elements to the act of surrender. However, surrender begins with faith and trust. In most relationships, trust is something that is built over time but in this case–in the case of surrender to Jesus–it's a choice that we make often without requiring Jesus to necessarily prove Himself. Why? Well, mostly because He has ALREADY proven Himself. He's proven His love and faithfulness by dying for us. But true surrender doesn't happen because we're convinced to do it in our head; it happens because the Holy Spirit works in our heart and draws us in. A person is moved to surrender usually because the Holy Spirit has caused a sudden supernatural awakening in their heart of Who God really is and how He has already loved us. It's like we suddenly realize we've known Him all along–like a long-lost love. We are awakened to His deep love for us which causes us to fall in love with Him in response. That is surrender. Now, what is repentance?

Some think that repentance simply means to feel bad or feel remorse about something but it's much more than that. We see the word *repent* in various places in the New Testament. Matthew 3:1-2 says, "In those days John the Baptist came preaching in the wilderness of Judea, and saying, "Repent, for the kingdom of heaven is at hand!" Peter gave a discourse at Solomon's porch to all the people around them who were amazed at the healing of a lame man, "Repent therefore and be converted, that your sins may be blotted out, so that times of refreshing may come from the presence of the Lord…" (Acts 3:19). Repentance is a sudden awareness that you're going in the wrong direction and a decision to turn around and head back to God. It is also a decision to change one's mind on a matter–to decide to think differently. This is not just something we're called to do when we first believe but do on an ongoing basis. In Revelation chapters 2 and 3, we see Jesus calling the seven churches to repentance, so it's for those who are already on the journey in the church, not just those who are being converted.

Before I was converted at my sister's home, I really struggled with the thought that I was a sinner–that I was somehow guilty. But in that final moment before conversion, it all became very clear. I hadn't done anything heinous; I hadn't intentionally hurt anyone, but I knew that it was not just about what I had or hadn't done. It was more about who I was at my core–about my identity. It was about me not being holy like God is holy. And it was such a relief, that I didn't even know I needed, to finally be able to admit my sin and release the hidden shame connected to it. It was like I was finally able to come out of hiding and be honest about who I really was.

In the religion I grew up in we were always encouraged to make the confession, "I'm perfect and eternal." But deep down I knew the "I'm perfect" part was not true! I knew that was a lie. I was far from it! So much freedom came when I could be completely transparent with myself and God, admitting my sin. Plus, I finally felt the love of God in my heart and His presence so near to me. It was amazing!

What about you? Do you or did you have trouble seeing yourself as a sinner? For some of us, we've been through the ringer. We've had a rough life, and we've acted out in ways that clearly were not good. For others, they grew up in church and did the right thing for most of their life. There's nothing on their "rap sheet." They don't even know what a "rap sheet" is! How easy is it for someone who grew up in a sheltered environment with most of what they needed, see their need to repent before God? It takes an awakening from the Holy Spirit to take the veil off their eyes to see that even though they've been "good," they've not been God. They have not been and are not holy in any way. Understand friends, holiness is the "benchmark"—it is the "plumb line" to which we need to measure ourselves.

I am reminded about the story of the rich, young ruler, found in Mark 10:17-22, who asked Jesus what the one thing was he needed to do to gain eternal life. Jesus told him to sell all he had and give the proceeds to the poor, then come back and follow Him. The rich, young ruler did not like His answer and did not do what he was told; his riches had a hold of his heart. They were too important to him, so he left sad, without the hope of eternal life. Jesus follows this up by saying to His disciples the following:

> "Children, it is next to impossible for those who trust in their riches to find their way into God's kingdom. It is easier to stuff a rope through the eye of a needle than for a wealthy person to enter into God's kingdom." (TPT)

And it's this very truth that concerns me today for those in the western church. I don't believe Jesus was only talking about material wealth but also an assumed wealth of spirit that does not perceive its need nor their sin. In many countries across the globe, there is hardship and persecution untold and becoming a Christ follower is costly. It takes great courage, passion, love for Jesus, commitment, and resilience to follow Christ. Here in the western world, we don't have that extreme pressure, and so we are complacent. We say we are Christ followers, but our lives don't look much different than those in the world and I believe it's because we are not passionately in love with Jesus. So, I challenge you today friends, are you truly a Christ follower and are you doing and taking the commands of Christ seriously? Does the fire of Christ and a "yes" to Him burn in your heart? If not, I encourage you to recommit yourself to follow Christ with ALL of who you are. Leave nothing on the table.

As the Holy Spirit pulled back the curtain of my heart that day at my sister's home, I saw the ugliness there. I saw the lack, the emptiness of what truly mattered, but I also saw what Jesus offered. I saw His holiness, His love, and the hope that was in Him, and I grabbed hold of it. I humbled myself, admitted my need and became His daughter by His mercy, grace and love. Here's the good news for you: All of this—the mercy, grace, and unconditional love is available for you as well! No one is excluded—not the good, the bad, or the horrific. It doesn't matter where you've been, what you've done or how someone else has violated you; you are invited to come back into the Father's embrace.

Mercy, grace, and unconditional love is available for you!

There is no sin that is too great for God. No sin is too terrible for God, and no pit is too deep for Him to rescue whoever needs rescued. He's just waiting for those who will respond to His invitation of love—to come back home to His mighty arms of grace and protection.

Will you respond today?
Will you trust that God is that good?
Will you make Him Lord of your life today?

If you've already accepted the gospel of Jesus, will you consider that perhaps you've not surrendered all? Have you let God be Lord in your life? Have you considered what His desire is for your occupation, work life, love life, and family life? If not, I encourage you today, to trust Him. His plan and purposes are always for us and not against us and always have our best interest at heart. And don't think that if you surrender all, that means you must be single, or a missionary in some impoverished country, be poor, or live without nice things. No! That is not God's heart. Yes, some are called to be missionaries, but some are also called to the marketplace–to work in regular jobs and careers–to be light in worldly places. And it is absolutely fine to have nice things, as long as those nice things don't have you or have a grip on your heart. Trust Him to connect the dots for you. He created you and He knows exactly how to bless you and cause you to thrive perfectly.

Will you pray with me? If so, bring your heart into agreement with your words and pray from your heart:

> "Lord, Jesus, I recognize now that I need You. I recognize that I have fallen short of Your holiness, and I have sinned. I am sorry and I repent. I thank You today that You saw my need and pursued me in Your love. I thank You that You have made a way for me to be with You and to have eternal life–that You took my sin upon Yourself, died a horrible death to pay the price of my sin, and rose again victoriously over all the power of death and the evil one. I receive Your forgiveness; I receive Your gift of salvation, and I surrender my life and my heart to You fully. I give You control, Lord. I hold nothing back. You have captured my heart, and I trust You completely. In Jesus' name, amen."

Wow! God is good. There is a celebration in heaven right now over your decision either to accept Jesus for the first time or to completely surrender to His Lordship. Welcome to the journey of becoming all God created you to be!

3

Saved and Empowered

In many ways, we are powerless before surrendering to Jesus and His Spirit–powerless at least in the type of power that truly matters. The Bible tells us that we are actually dead to God before being saved and before being surrendered. Ephesians 2:1-3 in the Passion Translation says:

> "And his fullness fills you, even though you were once like corpses, dead in your sins and offenses. It wasn't that long ago that you lived in the religion, customs, and values of this world, obeying the dark ruler of the earthly realm who fills the atmosphere with his authority, and works diligently in the hearts of those who are disobedient to the truth of God. The corruption that was in us from birth was expressed through the deeds and desires of

our self-life. We lived by whatever natural cravings and thoughts our minds dictated, living as rebellious children subject to God's wrath like everyone else."

Even though we were spiritually powerless, we didn't feel it—we didn't realize it until the moment of salvation when it became abundantly clear. Unfortunately for many there was a different type of powerlessness that we did feel. We felt it deep . . . deep in our core because of mistreatment, unjust circumstances or perhaps neglect and abuse. Maybe you know what I'm talking about. Perhaps you were one of the ones who felt trapped in a hellish prison. I've known some of that and my heart goes out to you. The good news is there's healing for every injustice you've suffered found in Jesus AND there's salvation for our lost soul found at the cross. We are born again when we come to Jesus and make Him Lord of our lives and we become His sons and daughters, fully alive in Him, positionally sanctified in Him.

What does it mean to be positionally sanctified? Well, "sanctified" according to *Oxford Languages* on Google means:

- To set apart as or declared holy; consecrated.
- To make legitimate or bound by religious sanction.
- Freed from sin; purified.

Positionally sanctified means to be set apart before God making us able to stand before Him pure and holy (regardless of whether we are walking it out perfectly or not). This means that when we boldly go to the throne of grace before Father God in prayer, which we are invited to do,[2] God does not see sin, He sees the righteousness of Jesus which has been graciously given to us as a gift.[3] Isaiah 61:10 gives us a great prophetic word helping us to see this righteousness from God, as a robe we wear:

> "I will greatly rejoice in the LORD, my soul shall be joyful in my God; For He has clothed me with the garments of salvation, He has covered me with the robe of righteousness, as a bridegroom decks himself with ornaments, and as a bride adorns herself with her jewels."

When we first get saved, the robe may feel too large. We may not fill it out properly as our daily walk in this world may not be fully righteous. This is normal. Wear it anyway! Believe the truth that you DO have right standing before God *despite* your missteps. Your missteps will get fewer and farther between as you journey with the Lord. As long as your heart is to get there—you will get there by God's grace. One of the amazing things about God is that He believes in you! Why do I say this? Because God gives you and me everything up front as a gift without having to earn it and *then* He teaches us how to walk it out day by day. So, we are <u>positionally</u> sanctified, in the Spirit realm before God, but we also enter a <u>process</u> of being sanctified or perfected in our daily lives here and now—in our heart

---

[2] Hebrews 4:16, "Let us therefore come boldly to the throne of grace, that we may obtain mercy and find grace to help in time of need."

[3] II Cor. 5:21, "For He made Him who knew no sin to be sin for us, that we might become the righteousness of God in Him."

attitudes, our thinking, and our behaviors. Is your heart submitted to God? Is it humble? Is it teachable? Wonderful! You're on the way to fitting into your robe of righteousness well. The key to your advancing in sanctification or said more simply, changing your behavior so it reflects holiness, is BELIEVING who God says you are.

> Your belief about who you are determines how you will act.

Many Christians think that they need to change their behavior by pulling up their own bootstraps–by doing better by their own will and in their own power but nothing can be further from the truth. Your behavior is determined by who you think you are. If you believe that even after being saved, you're a no-good loser and sinner, you will act like a no-good loser and sinner. It is true that before being saved, you were a sinner, but now, by God's grace, you are a saint.[4] You may be a saint that is still working with the Lord to break a habit of sin, but that does not make you a "sinner." The term "sinner" speaks about identity and "sinner" is your OLD identity that was dealt with, once and for all, at the cross. It's done. It's finished. You <u>were</u> a sinner, and you were saved by grace. NOW you are a saint that occasionally struggles with sin, but you are getting brighter

---

[4] In many places in the New Testament believers are referred to as saints. See Romans 12:13, Romans 15:25, Phil. 4:21&22, II Cor. 9:1 and more.

and more like Jesus every day, as you submit to God's leading and empowerment.

Our words are important friends. They frame and create our experience.[5] It seems like a minor distinction, whether we are a "sinner" or we "have sin" but it's not; it's important. We absolutely need to speak the truth about our new identity in Christ and own it with confidence and boldness. You are not your own any longer; you were bought at a price. You belong to Christ (I Cor. 6:19-20). God calls you a saint, not because of anything you've done but because of everything Christ has done for you.

When you believe you are the righteousness of God, you are empowered to BE righteous.

Being saved and surrendered empowers us and enables us to sense the love of God for us individually. Right believing also empowers us and enables us to experientially know the love of God. What else do we need so we are empowered and enabled to sense God's love in our lives? Well, we need the fullness and empowering of the Holy Spirit which means we need the BAPTISM of the Holy Spirit.

John the Baptist said in Matthew 3:11, "I indeed baptize you with water unto repentance, but He who is coming after me is mightier than I, whose sandals I am not

---

[5] Proverbs 18:21, "Death and life are in the power of the tongue, and those who love it will eat its fruit."

worthy to carry. He will baptize you with the Holy Spirit and fire."

In John 20, the first time Jesus appears before the disciples as a group after His resurrection, He imparts the Holy Spirit to them, commissioning them as *Sent Ones*. He says in verse 21, "Peace to you! As the Father has sent Me, I also send you." Then verse 22 says, "And when He had said this, He breathed on them, and said, "Receive the Holy Spirit," and the disciples received the Holy Spirit. But . . . apparently, they needed something more because Acts 1:4-5 & 8 says this:

> "[4-5]And being assembled together with them, He commanded them not to depart from Jerusalem, but to wait for the Promise of the Father, "which," He said, "you have heard from Me; for John truly baptized with water, but you shall be baptized with the Holy Spirit not many days from now." [8]But you will receive power when the Holy Spirit comes on you; and you will be my witnesses in Jerusalem, and in all Judea and Samaria, and to the ends of the earth."

The word translated "power" in verse eight in the original language is "dynamis" pronounced doonamis. This means *raw power, strength, might, the ability to perform miracles* and is where we get the English word "dynamite" from. It is <u>explosive</u> power. And it is only at the "baptism" of the Holy Spirit when they received this power. They received the person of the Holy Spirit prior when Jesus breathed on them in John 20, but they did not receive the power of the Holy Spirit until the baptism.

We see the fulfillment of Acts 1:8 not long after during the Feast of Pentecost in Acts 2, when they were all gathered in one room. The Holy Spirit came upon them in power causing them all to speak in other languages.

The disciples received the Holy Spirit twice—once for their re-birth unto salvation and once in baptism for the complete infilling and outward soaking in His presence and power (think drinking a glass of water compared to jumping in a pool). We too need to be completely empowered through the baptism of the Holy Spirit so we can discern His presence and know His love in our heart.

How do we receive the baptism of the Holy Spirit? We simply posture our heart before the Lord and ask Jesus to do it for us. Remember back in Matthew 3:11, John said that Jesus would baptize us in the Holy Spirit? So ask Him! And be willing to receive. You can receive the baptism when you're alone with God in prayer, or you can receive right now as you're reading this, or you can receive from an anointed person of God laying hands on you. They are all valid ways to receive. But the Holy Spirit is in charge. He knows the right time for you to experience His power. Matthew 7:7-11 reminds us that those who ask, receive, and those who seek, find. And when we ask for bread, we're not going to be given a stone. When we ask for a fish, we're not going to be given a snake. So, we can be sure that when we ask for more of the Holy Spirit, we will receive more of the Holy Spirit, and nothing counterfeit.

With the Holy Spirit empowering the apostles in the New Testament, they did amazing things. They were baptized in the Holy Spirit at Pentecost and then continued to do the work of the ministry, boldly preaching the Word and healing people just like Jesus did. Jesus told us the following, in John 14:12:

> "Very truly I tell you, whoever believes in me will do the works I have been doing, and they will do even greater things than these, because I am going to the Father."

Unfortunately, we're not walking in those things... miracles, signs, and wonders, nor do we see them very often in our churches here in the western world. Jesus said in Luke 10:19, "Behold, I give you the authority to trample on serpents and scorpions, and over all the power of the enemy..." But it seems we are powerless despite what the scriptures say. We need to ask ourselves why! I believe we've not understood the Holy Spirit nor how He moves. I believe we've been afraid of a counterfeit move and thus shut Him down in the process. I also believe the institutionalization of the western church, the box we've created for it, has removed its power. We've created something that feels "safe," in our comfort zones and something we can control, but unfortunately, it doesn't bring transformation in people's lives very often–at least not the same type of transformation we see happening in the New Testament church. We've created a manageable system that lacks the power needed to change us and change our world. We need to know the Holy Spirit. We need to understand Who He is, how and where He functions, what His purpose is, and we need to trust Him as God.

4

Holy Spirit

When I first became a Christian, I was told that the Holy Spirit is the power of God. That made me think of the Holy Spirit as a force, a thing, and so I thought of the Holy Spirit as an "it." But this thinking is not accurate. Yes, it's true that the Holy Spirit is the One that gets things done, but He is a person. He is the third person of the trinity and therefore should be referred to as a "Him" just like you would refer to Father God or Jesus.

Ephesians 4:30 says, "And do not grieve the Holy Spirit of God, by whom you were sealed for the day of redemption." Isaiah 63:10 also talks about grieving the Holy Spirit. Grief is a feeling. If the Holy Spirit can grieve—if He can experience feelings at all, He must be a personality or in more common terms, a person. Obviously, not a person like you and I, but holy and supreme... God.

To help us understand the trinity better, think of a construction project. In such a project, you have the architect–the one who comes up with the ideas, the plans, and the blueprints. Then you have the foreman who, in the beginning, is "boots on the ground" getting the workers organized and oversees the project. Next you have the workers that stay on the jobsite and exert the raw power needed to get the job done. Father God is the Architect. Jesus is the Foreman. Holy Spirit is the worker. Holy Spirit is "hands on" with us. He's here on the earth getting the job done, connecting us to heaven.

Next, let's think about who we are. We were created in the image of God so our overall design should give us a clue about God's design. We are primarily a spiritual being. Now, we very often think of ourselves as just physical because that is what is obvious–it's what we can see, but we are not primarily a physical being; we are primarily spiritual.

I remember going to my great aunt Elsie's funeral when I was young and I was struck by how she looked. They had an open casket funeral service which I had never been to before and Aunt Elsie's body lay there ... still ... her face white as white could be, and I thought with puzzlement, *that's not my Aunt Elsie*. To me it didn't look like her at all. It was a strange feeling and experience, but I sensed even as a young girl, that the REAL Aunt Elsie was gone; she was not there and all that was left was an empty shell with no meaning and zero life.

We are primarily a human spirit, who has a soul which consists of our mind, will and emotions and we live in a body; in many places in scripture, Paul calls our body a "tent" pointing out that it is only a temporary dwelling (in its current condition). We are three parts yet one–spirit, soul, and body. We are very similar to God in form–three in one. Just as at the center of who we are, we are a "spirit being," God is also a "spirit being" and the Holy Spirit is His Spirit Who is completely equal in holiness, authority, pre-eminence, sovereignty, and importance to Father God and Jesus–just as worthy of our praise, worship, and honor.

In many places in John (14:26, 15:26, 16:7) the Holy Spirit is called "the Helper." In John 16:13, He is also called the "Spirit of truth" as follows:

> "However, when He, the Spirit of truth, has come, He will guide you into all truth; for He will not speak on His own authority, but whatever He hears He will speak; and He will tell you things to come. He will glorify Me, for He will take of what is Mine and declare it to you."

Here's what we need to understand about Holy Spirit: He is not neutered; He is not without power. On the other hand, we have the church. The church many times seems to be neutered. As we've already discussed, we don't see the power of God moving in the church very much anymore. But if the church is without power, it has neutered itself. The Holy Spirit is still very much full of supernatural power just as He was in the Bible. He has not lost His power in any way. So why is Holy Spirit not moving powerfully in our churches or in our lives? I believe the answer to this is three-fold: dishonor, lack of trust in Him, and lack of submission to Him.

The Holy Spirit is God and deserves to be honored as such. But we dishonor the Holy Spirit when we don't give Him room to move, when we try to control Him, when we disobey Him, when we shut Him down, when we would rather do things without Him in our own power our own way, when we try to tell Him what to do and what not to do, when we ignore His leading, when we don't trust Him, and when we leave Him out of our plans especially in the work of the ministry. We seem to think we can pick and choose how we want God to show up for us, but we can't. We don't have that right.

Yup, Holy Spirit's work can be unpredictable. When we don't know Him and when we're not tuned into His voice, we're not quite sure what to expect and that makes us nervous. Doesn't it? We are a people who like to plan ahead and control things. But we need the Holy Spirit! He is the One Who heals. He's the One Who draws people in. He's the One Who opens the eyes of the pre-believer and the One Who saves. He's the One Who backs you up when you stand against the enemy in your life. He's the power source! He's the One we need to be plugged into. Without Him we can do nothing of worth so we absolutely, without a doubt, need to trust Him, yield to Him and be obedient to what He says.

The Holy Spirit is the raw power of God. He is the One that causes supernatural manifestations that shift and change things in the natural realm. How do you feel about that? Does it make you uncomfortable when you see or experience something that is beyond explanation? If we feel His power like a warm blanket of comfort, that's great. We like that. Don't we? But when He causes us to fall to the floor, shake or weep like a baby, we don't like that so much because perhaps it's embarrassing or perhaps it makes us feel like we're not in control. Even though it may feel uncomfortable to our flesh, when the Holy Spirit moves on us in power, He is bringing deep healing that we need desperately, and the best part is we will feel much better when the work is done. Friends, it's pride and fear that keep us resisting His work and we must kick pride and fear to the curb. Where fear is concerned, I believe it is specifically the following:

- Fear of the supernatural
- Fear of the counterfeit
- Fear of not being in control
- Fear of being hurt or disappointed
- Fear of discerning things wrong
- The fear of man (other people)
  - Fear of looking weird or stupid
  - Fear of judgement
  - Fear of being labeled a "Jesus Freak"
  - Fear of not fitting in
  - Fear of being different
  - Fear of not being liked by others

Fear is not of God! Fear is the enemy. "For God has not given us a spirit of fear, but of power and of love and a sound mind" (II Timothy 1:7).

Yes, there have been abuses of the manifestation gifts (1 Cor. 12:7-11) of the Spirit in Charismatic churches.

Absolutely! There have been misuses and people have been hurt. People have faked falling out, exaggerated things for publicity's sake, prophesied inaccurately and more. I'm sorry if you've been hurt by it. I'm REALLY sorry! But I'm going to ask you to forgive. Please don't blame the Holy Spirit; it's not His fault. You know, people are dumb sometimes. We're just really dumb sheep at times! People are broken and do weird things because they want to look good in front of others or they're super passionate about what they want so they manufacture stuff or mis-discern the Lord. Please just forgive. Forgive those who have been misguided and move on. Don't throw the baby out with the bath water. Please. That is a mistake. We need the Holy Spirit and all His gifts in operation correctly, with integrity. It's a process to learn! If you've ever tried to discern the Spirit's voice, you know, so, please have grace for us all.

There does also, however, seem to be an unwritten social code that wants to control us—a lie that says certain behaviors are not acceptable. It's acceptable for us to cheer and holler at a sports game but not at church. And there IS a judgement in the church that needs to stop. "Oh, there's that Barb again—hoot'n and holler'n, make'n a scene, drawing attention to herself. She's some kind of Charismaniac. Can't control herself in church." Oh brother! Stop. It. Everyone is different! Everyone expresses themselves differently and news flash—the Lord loves it when we're willing to step out of the box to praise Him with vigor! Amen? He blesses those who aren't afraid to be passionate for Him, and I know you know it too. So, let's do something different! Let's break out in celebration. Let's do something we've not done before; perhaps we'll access a new level of glory and presence that will bring healing to our weary soul.

Back to fear and pride. Friends, they are not serving us! They are only keeping us stuck in bondage and oppression. It's time to take a risk and let the supernatural power of God heal us from the inside out no matter what that looks like. Are you with me? Will you choose to trust Holy Spirit today?

If so, bring your heart into agreement and pray with me:

> "Lord, I repent for not trusting Your Holy Spirit. I repent for disobeying Him, not honoring Him, and for walking in fear and pride, for not allowing Him to do the work He needs to do. I repent for resisting Your power, healing, and transformation. Please forgive me. I renounce pride, fear of the supernatural, fear of the counterfeit, fear of not being in control and the fear of man. I renounce dishonor toward Holy Spirit, and I command these things to leave me now, in Jesus' name. Holy Spirit, come and fill me afresh. I submit and yield to You now. Begin a new work in me today! Amen."

5

Journey to Wholeness

Once we have made the decision to accept Jesus, surrender to His Lordship, and trust the Holy Spirit, we begin a journey of inner healing and transformation. Many have thought their decision to believe and surrender simply marks the end of being without God and they now just wait to go to heaven, but instead it's actually a beautiful beginning–the beginning of healing and becoming all that God originally intended.

You see God had a vision of each of us before our creation. He had an idea of you and me–how He would gift us, what talents and abilities He would give us, what we would be passionate about, how we would uniquely touch the world around us and express ourselves, what color our hair and eyes would be–all of it. He had a plan. He created a blueprint and His blueprint was perfect.

Then there came a time for each of us to be released into the world. . . through the womb of our birth mother. Unfortunately, as Romans 5[6] says, because the world was contaminated with sin through Adam and Eve's disobedience, as soon as we enter the womb the contamination of the world begins to distort God's creation, and we are then born with challenges and distortions of God's design. For example, I was born with a predisposition toward rejection because I was rejected in the womb. I was born with a lot of fear and trauma which was passed on to me from my mother.[7] This is why it's very important for us to partner with God on this journey of healing and transformation through a relationship with Him, through prayer, and understanding our power and authority in Christ. This is also why it's very important to pray over your baby while he/she is in the womb, declaring the protection and mercy of God over them. Reading and declaring Psalm 139 over them is very powerful.

This journey that the Lord takes us on, beautifully reforms us. It undoes many things that were not God's best for us, and it reshapes us back the way God wanted us in the first place. Sometimes it's painful. Sometimes we need

---

[6] "Therefore, just as through one man sin entered the world, and death through sin, and thus death spread to all men, because all sinned–" (Romans 5:12 NKJV) "For as by one man's disobedience many were made sinners, so also by one Man's obedience many will be made righteous." (Romans 5:19 NKJV)

[7] A study on Epigenetics will verify the transference of emotional trauma through the genes.

to face some things head on, that we've been trying to hide or run from. But it is always worth the temporary discomfort.

When we break a bone and don't get it properly set, it "heals" awry, out of alignment and we end up experiencing pain for the rest of our lives. If we want to get it corrected later, the doctor will need to re-break the bone and set it properly so it can heal correctly. This ensures we don't have long-term pain. Well ... there may be things in our lives that are similar. Almost all of us have experienced adversity and/or affliction of some kind in this sin-ridden world and many times, the "healing" that has occurred over time, perhaps using worldly resources, is flawed. It's not perfect. Something doesn't get set in order or alignment in a timely manner; maybe there was a lie that didn't get exposed, and the "healing" of that trauma ends up being inadequate. Perhaps we experience on-going chronic pain as a result. But God's healing of trauma is always perfect and always complete. So, sometimes God needs to touch something (that you thought was done) or break something again so He can heal it His way–the way that will keep you well for the rest of your life. He is not a Band-Aid solution kind of God. Jesus does everything with excellence, with your best interest in mind. He wants you well and healthy in every way.

So, what scriptures tell us about this journey of transformation? In Philippians 2:12 Paul exhorts the church saying:

> "My beloved ones, just like you've always listened to everything I've taught you in the past, I'm asking you now to keep following my instructions as though I were right there with you. *Now you must continue to make this new life fully manifested* as you live in the holy awe of God–which brings you trembling into his presence" (TPT, emphasis added).

In other words, Paul is saying, now that you have this new life, you must live it out. You must live like you are saved and holy. Regarding the same theme, Paul exhorts the Corinthian church in 2 Corinthians 3:18 by saying the following:

> "We can all draw close to him with the veil removed from our faces. And with no veil we all become like mirrors who brightly reflect the glory of the Lord Jesus. We are being transfigured into his very image as we move from one brighter level of glory to another. And this glorious transfiguration comes from the Lord, who is the Spirit" (TPT).

We learn here that this transformation we are invited into is a work of the Spirit and not something we do in our own strength. We are not expected to pull up our own bootstraps. We rely on the Spirit and partner with what He is doing in us. He transforms us from one level of glory to another, making us brighter and brighter until we reflect the image of Christ. But our pursuit of the Spirit and our cooperation with Him is key to our progress.

Further, Paul speaks on the same theme in Romans 12:1-2 as follows:

> "Beloved friends, what should be our proper response to God's marvelous mercies? To surrender yourselves to God to be his sacred, living sacrifices. And live in holiness, experiencing all that delights his heart. For this becomes your genuine expression of worship. Stop imitating the ideals and opinions of the culture around you, but be inwardly transformed by the Holy Spirit through total reformation of how you think. This will empower you to discern God's will as you live a beautiful life, satisfying and perfect in his eyes" (TPT).

Here we learn that a further key to transformation is to change the way we think. Do you remember what we said about repentance on page 9? Repentance means to change one's mind. So, it's *repentance* that leads you in the transformation of your heart and life.

In my experience, there are many things that can hinder us from advancing in our journey of transformation. However, since our focus for this book is the love of God, we will focus on five that hinder us from receiving and sensing the love of God. (For a comprehensive study of a host of other hindrances, please pick up my book *Position Yourself for Healing* from Amazon) We will consider the stumbling blocks of self-protection, hard-heartedness and cold-heartedness, self-idolatry, and fear and pride (as they relate to more than just the manifestation of the Spirit's power).

6

Stumbling Blocks Removed

As I begin this key chapter, I'm reminded that in Bible times when a King was scheduled to visit a town, the workers of the town would prepare the road ahead of time so that the King would have a smooth journey in. They would groom the road and remove any large debris or stones, making it as smooth as possible. This is why the prophecy about Jesus' coming from Isaiah 40 was so poignant with John the Baptist. He was the one who fulfilled the prophecy before Jesus' first coming and now, we have servants of God operating in that same Spirit again, preparing the way for His second coming. Isaiah 40:3-4 reads as follows:

> "The voice of one crying in the wilderness: "Prepare the way of the LORD; Make straight in the desert a highway for our God. Every valley shall be exalted and every mountain and hill

brought low; the crooked places shall be made straight and the rough places smooth; the glory of the LORD shall be revealed, and all flesh shall see it together; for the mouth of the LORD has spoken."

As Jesus comes for us and we go out to meet Him, we don't want any debris on the road causing us to stumble or preventing Him from reaching us. Prepare the way of the Lord! Friends, our Jesus is coming back soon, so let's not delay in our preparation to meet Him.

As mentioned before, we may need to remove five big boulders that could be causing us to stumble and preventing us from receiving the love of God. They are as follows: self-protection, hard-heartedness or cold-heartedness, self-idolatry, fear, and pride.

What does removing a stone look like? Well, first it looks like repentance. We acknowledge that we are indeed struggling with that issue, and we ask the Holy Spirit to show us any way that we have partnered with sin because of it. We confess to God, and we choose to change our mind and turn away from it. We then renounce it, take authority over it, and command it to leave us and cease its operation in our life. In our prayer, we can ask the Holy Spirit to show us any woundedness in our heart that is connected and He will. We then can ask the Lord to heal the wounds of our heart as we forgive those who have contributed to the problem. As well, we can ask the Holy Spirit to show us if this is something that is <u>familiar</u> in our family's bloodline. Do you see it as a pattern through the generations? If so, you can confess it as an iniquity[8] in the family, repent on behalf of your ancestors and ask the Lord to cleanse your bloodline back and forward through the generations. Here, you are preventing the issue from being passed on to your children which is super powerful! (Get my book, *Spiritual Protection and Deliverance for our Children* from Amazon for more on this topic.) This process I've been describing to you is termed by some as *self-deliverance*. And boy is it powerful! And it works! As long as you mean it and pray in faith.

Here are a series of questions you can answer to help you know how to pray:

1. What is the possible issue? Is it a problem for you? (If so, confess to God.)
2. What other sin have you been entangled with that is connected? (confess it to God)
3. Is there a wound at the root of the issue? Did someone hurt you causing you to self-protect? (If yes, tell God about the wound, forgive the one who hurt you, and ask God to heal the wound with the blood of Jesus.)

---

[8] Iniquity is a bent of character, weakness, or propensity to sin in a certain way that is passed down through the generations. It only becomes sin in your life when you actually do it. Iniquity is in the bloodline because someone in the past four generations sinned in that way. So, fear can be an iniquity in your life, or it can be both, sin and iniquity; it depends if you've stumbled in it yet. We are to repent for both our sins and the iniquity (that the HS reveals to us) in our bloodline.

4. Has this issue become a stronghold in your life—something like a habit or addiction that you can't easily stop doing? (If so, <u>renounce</u> (verbally reject and divorce) the spirit of the issue, break its power and command it to leave you in Jesus' name. Remember Luke 10:19, Jesus has given you authority over <u>all</u> the power of the devil. Just make sure you go through all the previous steps first because you can't take authority over something you have not repented for.)
5. Is it a pattern in your family line? Can you see it in operation in the generation before you? (If so, confess it to God on behalf of your ancestors as "iniquity," repent on behalf of your family, renounce it and break its power, then ask God to cleanse your bloodline up and down with the blood of Jesus.)

Let's begin by talking about self-protection.

Self-Protection

Self-protection is when one decides that they are the only person they can count on, and they put walls around their heart for protection. It may present in various ways. Those ways may include the following:

- Being overly cautious of others
- Extreme independence
- Relying solely on oneself
- Not letting people in
- Expecting to get hurt by others
- Not connecting emotionally
- Not putting oneself "out there"

- Playing it safe
- Not trusting others
- Hiding oneself somehow
- Physically presenting oneself plainly so as not to be noticed (not wanting to draw attention to themselves)
- Not showing up socially
- Not recognizing and operating in one's gifts, calling, and talents
- Diminishing oneself
- Emotional coldness
- Pride, self-idolatry
- Easily angered
- Lowering expectations so we're not disappointed
- Not being able to receive care or help from others
- Holding opinions, thoughts, or ideas back so as not to be negatively judged or rejected
- Fear of rejection
- Fear of being judged

These are just some symptoms of self-protection; one person is not going to be doing all of them, but if any of them are present in your personality, I would strongly suggest you pray it out.

Why is self-protection a sin? That's a good question. It's a sin because God has promised to be our protection[9]

---

[9] "He stores up sound wisdom for the upright; He is a shield to those who walk uprightly; He guards the paths of justice, and preserves the way of His saints" (Prov. 2:7-8). "He who dwells in the secret place of the Most High shall abide under the shadow of the Almighty. I will

and if we're protecting ourselves, we're not trusting God. Plus, there is a reason a person is self-protecting and it's usually because they have been hurt by someone they trusted. This means there are many things connected to it, like anger, a sense of betrayal, woundedness, and unforgiveness. Many times, we have carried pain and unforgiveness toward someone for a long time. All this needs to be confessed as sin. Yes, you may have been hurt by the sinful actions of someone else, but our reaction to people's sin, no matter how justified you think it is, very often is sinful. If you've already prayed through the <u>root cause</u> of self-protection, kudos to you! But now pray through and release the tendency to not trust God and protect yourself.

As I listed the above symptoms of self-protection, I realized that the remaining four "stones" possibly preventing us from receiving the love of God, cold/hard-heartedness, pride, self-idolatry, and fear, are all connected and are a <u>result</u> of self-protection or the <u>wound</u> causing self-protection. You may have noticed them in the list too. I encourage you to prayerfully consider the list and ask the Holy Spirit to put His finger on the ones you need to pray through. I also encourage you to include some sort of physical act that represents the removal of these stones. Perhaps you find five stones, write on them the initials of the symptom you're removing and as you pray, throw them as hard as you can into a lake or pond or into a corn field,

---

say of the LORD, 'He is my refuge and my fortress; My God, in Him I will trust'" (Ps. 91:1-2).

anywhere where you won't hurt someone (lol). (Don't be like my twin boys when they were young who thought it would be fun to have a rock fight. Ouch.) Adding a physical act to your prayer reinforces it and puts legs to your faith. It's powerful. It helps you to really mean what you say when you engage your physical body and all your senses. Also, please pray out loud. Yes, you can pray in your heart at times, but not this time. Your words need to be spoken out loud for every spirit in the atmosphere to hear what you are doing and releasing yourself from. It is a spiritual warfare strategy must! Trust me on this one, my friend.

I am going to provide a prayer, but you <u>must</u> decide in your heart first that you are <u>done</u> with these behaviors and that you want to be free. You must <u>want</u> to be free, and you must bring your heart and your faith into agreement. And I'm going to say something simple yet extremely powerful right here . . . only <u>one</u> person can be on the throne of your heart, and it <u>must</u> be God! That means, YOU are going to have to get off the throne. You are going to have to finally decide to let God be God . . . let Him be Lord.

Here's an outline for prayer. Obviously feel free to add or take away from it (without losing any of the elements).

> "Lord, I confess that I have walked in agreement with self-protection, cold-heartedness, hard-heartedness, pride, self-

idolatry, fear, unforgiveness, bitterness and anger.[10] I repent.

God, I have been unkind, rude, arrogant, cold, disrespectful, dishonoring,
[list any way you have treated others with less than grace and kindness].
It was wrong and I repent. Please forgive me.

Lord, I choose to forgive
[say their names] for [say what they did to hurt you – be specific].
I release them all to You now.

Father, heal the wounds in my heart that were created by these injustices. Pour out Your healing oil and the blood of Your Son, Jesus, over every wound in my heart.
[take a moment to experience this; engage your spirit and see it happening by faith]
I don't want to hide these wounds anymore. And I don't want them to hurt anymore. Be my Healer, God. Thank You, Jesus. I receive Your forgiveness, God, and I receive Your healing.

Lord, I also confess that these sins are iniquities in my bloodline, and I ask You right now to cleanse my bloodline of these things up through the generations and down through

---

[10] Let all bitterness, wrath, anger, clamor, and evil speaking be put away from you, with all malice. And be kind to one another, tenderhearted, forgiving one another, even as God in Christ forgave you" (Eph. 4:31-32).

the generations of my descendants. [See on the screen of your imagination the blood of Jesus traveling through your ancestral bloodline, cleansing it from these issues.]

Finally, Lord, in the authority of Jesus, I renounce, reject, bind, and divorce myself from the spirits of self-protection, cold-heartedness, hard-heartedness, pride, self-idolatry, fear, unforgiveness, bitterness, and anger and I command them to leave me now upon my natural breathing and to never come back, in Jesus' mighty name.

[Breathe out and in faith believe they are leaving, simply because you told them to. You have that authority. They <u>must</u> comply.]

I close every door and sever every spiritual access point to these demonic spirits right now, in Jesus' name.

Holy Spirit come and fill me completely. Baptize me afresh in Your presence and power. Fill every space in me that has been swept clean and help me to walk in righteousness in Your power; help me to hear and know Your voice. I fully submit to You, in Jesus' mighty name, Amen."

That is deliverance friends! Praise the Lord! Way to go. Kudos to you for praying it all the way through. Now, however, you have the <u>responsibility</u> to partner with the

Holy Spirit to walk it out. You will need to get to know the Holy Spirit better so you can get to know His voice and the best way to do that is to read your Bible. Also, spend time in praise and worship every day, soaking in His presence and His love.

With those stumbling blocks removed, I declare that you are open and free to receive the truth of how much God truly loves you! I declare that the love of God is dropping from your head to your heart . . . from intellectual knowledge to heart knowledge and the experience of it will change you, overtake you, and bless you like you've never been blessed before.

7

Freedom in Christ

Living out your new-found freedom is now your mission, and the best tool to help you is the Word of God—specifically the scriptures that teach us who we have become in Christ.

I'm going to include part of a chapter from my previous book, *Spiritual Protection and Deliverance for our Children*, about who we have become in Christ. Please forgive me if this section seems repetitive, but it is vital foundational truth for you to stand on <u>every time</u> the enemy tries to feed you lies about your worth or identity.

Who Are You?

This may be a bit of a trick question but, "Who are you?" Think about that for a moment. How would you answer that question? I think most of us would answer with what we do, our occupation, what roles we fill and perhaps how many children we have, but that's not really *who* we are at our core. In fact, if we define ourselves by our occupation and roles, our identity becomes muddled and we become uncertain of who we are when we perhaps lose our job, change careers and when our roles in life shift, for instance when our children grow up, start their own lives and become independent. It can cause mothers, especially, to go through an identity crisis when they are no longer needed by their children. It is much better to define ourselves by what won't change—by the eternal aspects of who we are. With that in mind, I might answer, "I am Barbara Jane, daughter of the most-high God, Jehovah, younger sibling to Jesus Christ of Nazareth, blessed and highly favored, called to encourage the Bride of Christ to walk in everything Christ died to give her—salvation, freedom, and holiness." All who have surrendered their hearts to Jesus and accepted God's free gift of salvation can also claim their identity as a son or daughter of God. John 1:10-13 says:

> He was in the world, and the world was made through Him, and the world did not know Him. He came to His own, and His own did not receive Him. But as many as received Him, to them He gave the right to become children of God, to those who believe in His name: who were born, not of blood, nor of the will of the flesh, nor of the will of man, but of God.

As children of God, we have been re-born—born of the Spirit. In John 3, Nicodemus, a Pharisee, meets with Jesus in secret and tries to understand how one can be *born again*.

Beginning in verse 5 Jesus says to Nicodemus the following:

> "Most assuredly, I say to you, unless one is born of water and the Spirit, he cannot enter the kingdom of God. That which is born of the flesh is flesh, and that which is born of the Spirit is spirit. Do not marvel that I said to you, 'You must be born again.' The wind blows where it wishes, and you hear the sound of it, but cannot tell where it comes from and where it goes. So is everyone who is born of the Spirit." (John 3:5-8)

It's a bit of a mind bender, isn't it? By all appearances, nothing has changed, but it couldn't be further from the truth. Nicodemus struggled to understand it, and I think many of us do too.

When we are born in the natural, we are born of the flesh. Our flesh is formed, and our soul comes alive in the womb with the help of our Creator, but our spirit man inside is not alive to God; we are only flesh–completely and solely carnal. Because of the sin of Adam and Eve, every person born physically is born dead in spirit and disconnected from true life found only in God.[11] Our family is merely our natural family related by natural blood. But, when we surrender to Christ, a miracle takes place on the inside, in the invisible

---

[11]Genesis 2:16-17, "And the LORD God commanded the man, "You are free to eat from any tree in the garden; but you must not eat from the tree of the knowledge of good and evil, for when you eat from it you will certainly die" (NIV).

spiritual realm, and our spirit-man is re-born coming alive to God and connected eternally to His heart and Spirit. We become part of God's family connected by the blood of Jesus shed on our behalf. Second Corinthians 5:17 tells us that we are new creations in Christ—not creations that have been renovated or spruced-up but brand-new creations. The old is completely done away with and the new is here!

> Therefore, from now on, we regard no one according to the flesh. Even though we have known Christ according to the flesh, yet now we know him thus no longer. Therefore, if anyone is in Christ, he is a new creation; Old things have passed away; Behold, all things have become new. (2 Cor. 5:16-17).

Ephesians 2 also gives us great insight into how we have changed as children of God:

> [1]Once you were dead because of your disobedience and your many sins. [2]You used to live in sin, just like the rest of the world, obeying the devil—the commander of the powers in the unseen world. He is the spirit at work in the hearts of those who refuse to obey God. [3]All of us used to live that way, following the passionate desires and inclinations of our sinful nature. By our very nature we were subject to God's anger, just like everyone else. [4]But God is so rich in mercy, and he loved us so much, [5]that even though we were dead because of our sins, he gave us life when he raised Christ from the

dead. (It is only by God's grace that you have been saved!) ⁶For *he raised us from the dead along with Christ and seated us with him in the heavenly realms* because we are united with Christ Jesus. ⁷So God can point to us in all future ages as examples of the incredible wealth of his grace and kindness toward us, as shown in all he has done for us who are united with Christ Jesus.... ¹⁰For we are God's masterpiece. He has created us anew in Christ Jesus, so we can do the good things he planned for us long ago (Ephesians 2:1-7; 10 NLT, emphasis added).

It never gets old reading about how God has transformed us spiritually! He has raised us up with Christ and seated us in heavenly places with Him. Jesus sits at the right-hand of God and this scripture passage is telling us that we sit there with Him. Our lives are hidden in Christ! We are His body. We are in heavenly places with Him—not physically of course but spiritually speaking, we are. We are citizens of heaven (Philippians 3:20), Christ's ambassadors living on the earth re-presenting Him to the world (2 Cor. 5:20). And in Christ, we have become the righteousness of God (2 Cor. 5:21). We are a chosen generation, appointed, predestined to belong to Him, a royal priesthood, a holy nation, His own special people, bought at a price to belong to Him (1 Peter 2:9, 1 Cor. 6:20, Eph. 1:4-5).

The following is adapted from Neil T. Anderson's book, Victory Over the Darkness. In Christ, by His grace and mercy, we are the following:

- The salt of the earth (Matt. 5:13).
- The light of the world (Matt. 5:14).
- Children of God (John 1:12).
- Part of the true vine, a channel of Christ's life (John 15:1&5).
- Christ's friends (John 15:15).
- Chosen and appointed by Christ to bear His fruit (John 15:16).
- Slaves to righteousness (Romans 6:18).
- Enslaved to God (Romans 6:22).
- Sons and daughters of God; God is spiritually our Father (Romans 8:14-15; Galatians 3:26; 4:6).
- Joint heirs with Christ, sharing in His inheritance with Him (Romans 8:17).
- Temples of the Holy Spirit—dwelling places of God (1 Cor. 3:16; 6:19).
- United to the Lord and one spirit with Him (1 Cor. 6:17).
- Members of Christ's body (1 Cor. 12:27; Eph. 5:30).
- Reconciled to God and ministers of reconciliation (2 Cor. 5:18-19).
- Heirs of God (Gal. 4:6-7).
- Saints (1 Cor. 1:2; Eph. 1:1; Phil. 1:1; Col. 1:2).
- Prisoners of Christ (Eph. 3:1; 4:1).
- Righteous and holy (Eph. 4:24).
- Hidden with Christ in God (Col. 3:3).
- Expressions of the life of Christ because He is our life (Col. 3:4).

- Chosen of God, holy and dearly loved (Col. 3:12; 1 Thess. 1:4).
- Sons and daughters of light and not of darkness (1 Thess. 5:5).
- Holy partakers of a heavenly calling (Heb. 3:1).
- Partakers of Christ; we share in His life (Heb. 3:14).
- God's living stones being built up in Christ as a spiritual house (1 Peter 2:5).
- Aliens and strangers to this world in which we temporarily live (1 Peter 2:11 AMP).
- Children of God who will resemble Him when He returns (1 John 3:2).
- Complete in Christ (Col. 2:10).
- Overcomers (1 John 5:4, "For every child of God defeats this evil world, and we achieve this victory through our faith." NLT).
- Safe from harm—the devil cannot touch us (1 John 5:18, "We know that God's children do not make a practice of sinning, for God's Son holds them securely, and the evil one cannot touch them." NLT).

Because we are now Christ's own possession, we also have access to His victory over the devil and according to Luke 10:19, He has given us authority in Him to overcome all the power of the devil.

I pray that you are encouraged by that amazing list of truths about you... in Christ. None of it is true because of what you have done. We cannot take any credit or glory.

Instead, it is ALL true purely because of Christ's sacrifice for us. It is all God's doing.

Here's the mystery in it all. We actually don't walk it out perfectly yet, do we? But we can still claim it as true RIGHT NOW, because God says it is true right now. God gives us *everything* up front (because of His amazing grace). He credits our identity as being pure and holy just like Jesus BEFORE we walk it out perfectly because He knows He can transform us into the image of His Son as we submit to Him. And He is already executing that plan in you and in me!

I choose to believe God's Word about me *despite* my periodic failures. What about you? Will you choose to believe it for yourself? God's Word is truth. Let's stand on it for ourselves and resist anything contrary to it.

There is power in believing the truth about yourself and declaring it out loud. It empowers you and sets you up to behave like the favored son or daughter that you are.

Many Christians struggle with their behavior. They can't seem to get out of a pattern of sin. Sometimes deliverance is needed but sometimes it's simply a matter of renouncing the lies they've believed about their identity. If they believe that they are a no good looser, they will act like a no good looser. But if they renounce those self-deprecating thoughts and believe the truth instead, they will begin to behave like the son or daughter that they are.

At the end of Romans 7, Paul describes what we all feel at times: a tug of war happening within us between the flesh and spirit. We do what we don't want to do, and we don't do what we ought to do, and it can feel frustrating. Thankfully, Paul reminds us in Romans 8:1-2 as follows:

> There is therefore now no condemnation to those who are in Christ Jesus, who do not walk according to the flesh, but according to the Spirit. For the law of the Spirit of life in Christ Jesus has made me free from the law of sin and death.

I find making the following declaration out loud over myself most helpful: "Because I am in Christ, I have been set free from the law of sin and death. It no longer has any more power over me. I am free to choose not to sin! I am free to choose holiness. I am free to do what is right."

Lastly, our struggle with the enemy is not a power struggle. We are on the same team with Jesus—God's team—so there is NO contest. Satan doesn't have a chance. No…

Our struggle against the devil is not about power; it's about truth and our boldness and willingness to stand on it.

"And you shall know the truth, and the truth shall make you free" (John 8:32). Rise up, daughter of God! It's time to stop allowing the enemy to lie to you and push you around. God is backing you up. Your Father is right behind you enforcing His victory through you.

Conclusion

Congratulations on completing this booklet and praying through your challenges! If you've attended one of our LoveFest gatherings, for which this booklet was originally written, whoop whoop! Thanks for being there! If you've not been to a gathering, please go to the website makeyourselfready.com to find out when our next one is and make sure you register.

Thank you so much for taking the time to glean from my writings and allowing me to speak into your life. I pray it has helped you and that you begin to experience healing and greater freedom emotionally and spiritually because of your obedience to the Lord in laying it all down and saying "yes" to Him. It does take great courage to face the real you on the inside–to dismantle the walls you've created for your own safety, and I celebrate your decision to do that. Honestly, any "safety" we create is false safety. The only true safety is found in Jesus. Amen? I pray you agree!

With that, I bless you and declare that true freedom is ringing loud and clear in your life. Keep going my friend! The Lord has so much more for you, and the best is yet to come! Much love to you.

About the Author

Barbara Jane grew up in a family of five attending a Christian Science church until the age of eighteen when she left home and at the age of twenty-two the Lord, Jesus, called her into His fold. She has now never been so grateful for the transformation the Lord began in her life in that moment of revelation and salvation. It was a moment when everything clicked into place, and everything she knew about God became crystal clear and made sense; the revelation of Jesus Christ was the missing piece. The years that followed would prove to be life altering and internally transforming in many ways.

Through her thirty-six years of faith in Christ thus far, she has had to face and renounce many things that tainted her family-line like the antichrist spirit, the spirit of error and deception, lies, abuse in many forms, deep anger, hate, unforgiveness, bitter judgements, vows to self, disappointment, rejection, self-loathing, and despair. As she has walked out of agreement with darkness, breakthrough has been had in different areas of life including her ability to conceive and bear natural children. Because of the goodness and healing of the Lord, Barbara Jane had four amazing children—one beautiful girl and three handsome boys, who are now all thriving adults. In addition, she and her husband now have a wonderful daughter-in-law who makes a lovely addition to their original four.

It is with great honor that Barbara Jane pours out to her readers the knowledge, wisdom, and understanding that the Lord has poured into her. And it is her prayer that the time, love, and effort she has put into her books brings about great blessing and transformation in the lives of others. There is nothing more gratifying to Barbara than being used of the Lord to assist the Bride of Christ in getting ready for her big day, finally becoming perfectly united with her bricegroom, Jesus Christ.

Barbara has written five other books you might be interested in. They are as follows:

Barren No More: Prayer Strategy for Every Believer Experiencing Fertility Challenges

Key to Fertility: Rewriting Your Stories for Success in Conceiving and Birthing Babies

Sweet Sorrow: Surviving the Emotional Waves of Releasing Your Son to His Bride

Position Yourself for Healing: Finding the Sweet Spot Where Healing Becomes Reality

Spiritual Protection and Deliverance for our Children

All car be purchased on Amazon.

References

Anderson, Neil T. *Victory Over the Darkness*. Bloomington, Minnesota: Bethany House, 2014.

Chapman, Gary. *The Five Love Languages: The Secret to Love that Lasts*. Chicago, Illinois: Northfield Publishing, 2024.

www.ingramcontent.com/pod-product-compliance
Lightning Source LLC
Chambersburg PA
CBHW070857050426
42453CB00012B/2246